Jah Rastafari
Rasta Beliefs & Way of Life

By

Empress Yuajah

Copyright © 2016 Empress Yuajah

All rights reserved.

ISBN: **10: 1530384923**

ISBN-13: **978-1530384921**

DEDICATION

To all the Kingman and Empress who trod the earth, and keep the faith. Jah Live. Blessed Love.

To My Readers:

I wrote this book to help those who want to gain a thorough understanding of what it means to be a Rasta, and to provide a solid springboard for those who want guidance on "how to" live the Rastafari Way of life.

I hope this book, provides all the answers to your questions and I hope it provides assurance that Rastafari is the rightful way of Jah, the Almighty creator.

Blessed Love, Rastafari.

Table of Contents

THE CHOICE OF RASTAFARI 8

IMPORTANCE OF KING SELASSIE I AND EMPRESS MENEN IN RASTAFARI 9

6 STEPS TO CONVERT TO RASTAFARI 25

HOW TO CHOOSE YOUR RASTA NAME 43

4 WAYS TO MEDITATE AS A RASTA 49

WHY ARE YOU A RASTA?

.... 57

4 PILLARS OF RASTAFARI HEALTH 59

ITAL FOOD AS RASTA 72

6 SPIRITUAL OBLIGATIONS OF RASTAFARI 85

BIBLE STUDY AS A RASTA
.... 94

WHITE RASTAFARI 100

THE MEANING OF DREADLOCKS AS A RASTA
.... 103

OVERSTANDING JAH ZION

& BABYLON 110

HOW TO RAISE A RASTA CHILD 116

FINDING A RASTA MENTOR 124

KING SELASSIE I SPEECHES 130

MY RASTA JOURNEY 144

MORE BOOK TITLES BY EMPRESS YUAJAH 150

THE CHOICE OF RASTAFARI

Rastafari has specially selected every Rasta, however that Rasta must also choose Rastafari to reap the rewards. It is a two way spiritual street. A Rasta man can be "powerful" or "weak" depending upon how deep he chooses to live and embrace the faith.

Every Rasta knows within themselves if their life is a Reflection of their spiritual beliefs that puts the will and the works of Jah first. When this happens the Rasta woman or Rasta man will be powerful, peaceful, confident and content.

Rastafari is a spiritual gift, if you want to see its power working in your life, you will have to work Rastafari in your life.

May you meet Jah on your Journey, May you know his might and his blessings. Rastafari, King Selassie I.

IMPORTANCE OF KING SELASSIE I AND EMPRESS MENEN IN RASTAFARI

As an aspiring Rasta, You may be wondering about the importance and meaning of King Selassie I and Empress Menen in the Rastafari faith. What role do they play? Why are they so important? The following is 5 reasons...

IMPORTANCE OF KING SELASSIE I AND EMPRESS MENEN IN RASTAFARI

#1 Royalty and Self Respect

The life and crowning of King Selassie I and Empress Menen in Rastafari, is *to demonstrate Royalty, Self Respect*

By the example set by the crowning and Relationship of King Selassie I and Empress Menen, Rasta maintain a *high standard* for ourselves in all things. From the clothing that we choose to wear, to the way we speak, the friendships we keep, and the way we choose to live and view our lives. Rasta emulates the life and standards of King Alpha and Queen Omega at all times.

How to Emulate "the King & Queen" as Rasta

King Selassie I is the Role Model for the Rasta man, and Empress Menen is the Role Model for the Rasta woman. Some of the ways we as Rasta Emulate the King and Queen are...

- Maintaining cordial relationships with others including those who we may consider "difficult to deal with" or whom we may consider to be our "enemies."
- Expressing Love and appreciation for our Kingman and Empress as *Creations of Jah*
- Speak using consideration for the sensitivity for hearts and minds others

IMPORTANCE OF KING SELASSIE I AND EMPRESS MENEN IN RASTAFARI

2 the Royal Lineage of King Solomon

Another reason King Selassie I is so important in Rastafari culture is to *put a face to the Royal Lineage of King Solomon.*

King Selassie I is the 225 direct descendent to sit up on the throne of King David, which was also occupied by *the wise King Solomon, who is King David's son.*

Rastafari Legend has it that, The Queen of Sheba and The Wise King Solomon made love and had a baby boy which was named Menilik, who became "King Menelik I." King Menilik had a son "King Menelik II," who is King Selassie I uncle. King Selassie I and King Menelik are of "the tribe of Judah," which is part of biblical Royal history, related to King Solomon.

As Rasta we pay our Respects to King Selassie I as the face of Jah, and all the ordained Kings of the Tribe of Judah.

IMPORTANCE OF KING SELASSIE I AND EMPRESS MENEN IN RASTAFARI # 3

#4 Royal energy in the home

As stated Earlier images of "the King and Queen" as Rasta are reminders of our own Royal Heritage. For this reason Rasta love to have images of the King and Queen in every room in thier home. Including Wall hangings, plaqued photos of the King and Queen, Rastafari mugs, clocks with the Kings face, framed speeches by King Selassie I etc. Rasta believe and feel these Royal images of the King Selassie I and Empress Menen brings positive spiritual Energy into the home and into our lives.

IMPORTANCE OF KING SELASSIE I AND EMPRESS MENEN IN RASTAFARI

#4 Demonstrate Positive history and Heritage

Another Reason Empress Menen and King Selassie I have so much importance in Rastafari culture is that they demonstrate positive African history and heritage.

King Selassie I and Empress Menen were crowned November 2nd 1930. As former slaves, black people have had a hard time in Babylon <u>recovering the whole truth about our heritage and our history.</u> Many black youth in school only learn that black people were *slaves.* Not much before black slavery and not much after black slavery, and not much about our <u>contributions</u> to society as a nation.

There were many photos taken of the life of the King and Queen. Jah ordained the crowning of King Selassie I and Empress Menen so that Black people have a *positive black role model couple (male and female)* after black slavery was abolished. All though the King and Queen are from Africa, and ruled over Ethiopia, in Rastafari, they represent positive role models ordained by Jah for all people of all Nations.

IMPORTANCE OF KING SELASSIE I AND EMPRESS MENEN IN RASTAFARI

5 Equality of the Sexes

In the Rastafari Livity, Men and Women are seen as equal, because, the same day

(November 2nd 1930) King Selassie I was crowned King of Ethiopia, Empress Menen was also crowned, Queen of Ethiopia during the same coronation.

King Selassie I is also known as "The King of Kings" and Empress Menen is also known as "The Queen of Queens" in Rastafari Culture.

IMPORTANCE OF KING SELASSIE I AND EMPRESS MENEN IN RASTAFARI

#6 Self Reliance & Legacy

The King and Queen through hard work and determination created a Legacy between them. King Selassie I created schools in his name, ...Because of this example Rasta also like to build things in our name that people can utilize positively and that carries the name of Rastafari for generations. Bob Marleys legacy was his music and his message. Through his work, he was also self reliant. He left a legacy for his children, and his children's children.

The Importance of King Selassie I and Empress Menen in Rastafari Re-cap

- Generate powerful positive energy through images and words of King Selassie I and Empress Menen displayed in the home
- Demonstrate positive African history and heritage, and positive African role models to Africans and the World
- Demonstrate what an image of self respect and dignity looks like in order for one to emulate it
- To put a face to the Royal lineage of King David and his son King Solomon
1. **Equality of the Sexes:** Teach Rasta equality of the sexes. Both King Selassie I and Empress Menen were crowned November 2nd 1930. King Selassie I as "King of Kings..." and

Empress Menen as "Queen of Queens..."
- **Self Reliance & Legacy:** The King and Queen demonstrate to Rasta to Create our own work

6 STEPS TO CONVERT TO RASTAFARI

Many people who want to embrace the faith of Rastafari wonder, "just how do I convert to Rastafari?" The answer is, there is no right or wrong way to *Convert to Rastafari.* As a Rastafari myself having taken my vow just 7 years ago, there was some inner spiritual things I did, coupled with some outer changes to my environment and lifestyle that helped me to convert my spiritual beliefs from Christianity to Rastafari.

6 STEPS TO CONVERT TO RASTAFARI

Step #1 - Clean out your refrigerator

When I made the decision to live as Rasta, the first thing I did was remove all cow's milk from my fridge and replace it with soya milk, and remove any meat and meat products. Eating four footed animals or any animal (dead) flesh, and drinking cows' milk is not a part of the Rastafari livity.

I realized after I stopped drinking cow's milk how much the aftertaste disturbed my palette and how much the cow's milk would bloat my stomach. I now use soya milk or almond milk for eating cereal, cooking, and just about anything else that calls for cow's milk.

Oh and if you have food that comes in a box in your freezer... throw that out too. Chances are it's full of preservatives that are unhealthy for the temple and cause weight gain, indigestion, and contribute to sickness of the holy temple in the long run.

Jah say "meat is not for Rasta"

As far as eating meat is concerned I didn't really have any meat in my fridge to have to throw out while I was converting to Rastafari because Jah wrote it on my heart when I was just 17 years old, that *dead flesh* is not fit for my holy temple to consume. I haven't consumed any meat or beef or pork since then. That was over 15 years ago.

6 STEPS TO CONVERT TO RASTAFARI
Step #2 Eat Fresh organic foods and dried foods for the temple

As a Rasta you will now buy your food fresh, each week for the week to come. Organic fruits and Vegetables are a must as a Rastafari. These foods give the temple, important vitamins and nutrients it needs to function at it best.

Consider buying some Organic dried fruit at your local health food store too. My favorite dried foods are peanuts, dried apples, dried banana chips, raisins, dried apricots, dried cranberries and some dried plantain chips. These are great for snacking *on the go* as Rasta, because we typically do not eat convenience store bought food out of packages, nor do we eat "fast food" such as Mc. Donald's or Burger King, or KFC etc, because they are processed, full of oil, and not part of The Rastafari Livity nor Ital.

6 STEPS TO CONVERT TO RASTAFARI

Step #3 Hang up your Lion of Judah flag in your home

It is important as you convert to Rastafari to see symbols of Rastafari in and around your home. To Rasta, a Lion of Judah flag hung in the home means "The King lives here."

As I was converting to Rastafari so to speak, my Lion of Judah flag really helped me to feel *more connected to the spirit of Rastafari*. The moment I hung it up over my bed, I noticed the spiritual energy in the room. I also felt more grounded... like *The King* was around me... available for guidance and support.

My good friend Ras Anbasa, has two Lion of Judah Flags. One in his home over his bed as well, and one hanging from his Balcony facing the street. We Rasta like to share our love of Rastafari with others, as we display symbols of Rastafari outside and inside of our home.

My Lion of Judah flag spans 5 feet by 3 feet. The Colors remind me of Africa and all the love Jah must have felt in his heart when he created the first man.

The Lion of Judah flag is also a *Royal Ethiopian Emblem, and tribal flag (Tribe of Juda)h*...It represents...

King Selassie I	Africa
	Hope

The Spiritual Self	Unity
Love	Royalty
Victory	Truth
Nature	Strength
Jah	Jah people

Rasta loves the lion of Judah flag. It is a worldwide symbol of Jamaica, Reggae Music, and Rastafari.

6 STEPS TO CONVERT TO RASTAFARI #4

More "Rasta Reggae Music"

Another thing I did to convert my home and my spiritual awareness to Rastafari, was to start buying and listening to more Rasta Reggae music. Since I listen to music on my laptop, I started buying more Reggae music off iTunes. I have such a wicked Rasta Reggae music collection now.

If you are unfamiliar with Rastafari Reggae music here is a list of artists to check out.

"Militant DJ Rasta Reggae"	"Singing Type of Rasta Reggae"
Sizzla	Dennis Brown
Capleton	Gregory Isaacs
Richie Spice	Luciano
I Wayne	Jah Cure
Anthony B	Bob Marley

| Queen Ifrica Jah 9 | Alborosie |

As a Rastafari I don't really listen to music by other artists who are not Rasta. Rastafari is an energy/Vibration. I keep other types of music that I listen to at a minimum, because I know words and sound have a power in them. I aim to develop and maintain a Rasta consciousness – not Babylon.

6 STEPS TO CONVERT TO RASTAFARI
Step #5

Seek Truth and Wisdom

The King James Version bible is Rastafari from cover to cover. However if you would like some Rastafari spiritual teachings as a new Rasta check out my book called "Rasta Bible: Rastafari spiritual wisdom" on amazon.com

Much of the wisdom that Rasta share comes from Jah and Jah teachings. The King James version bible is full of Jah

teachings. The bible is one of my very important tools as a Rasta Empress that I use to seek *truth and Wisdom.*
The bible includes teachings from the prophets who spoke with Jah personally, and provide truth about Life and how one should conduct himself concerning the desires of Jah.

Much of our wisdom as Rasta comes from learning from the ones before us.
Including black civil rights leaders, all Revolutionaries, Rasta Reggae Musicians... Etc.

Some popular Revolutionaries in Rastafari culture

Nelson Mandela
Ghandi
King Selassie I
Martin Luther King
Norman Manley
Nanny (of the Maroons)
Paul Bogle

To a Rasta, to seek truth and Wisdom means...

Investigating the whole story not just accepting one angle.

Read all food package labels before we decide to consume it.

Understanding that there is more truth that is hidden that truth that is revealed in most stories and situations

Studying history of all peoples of all nations including, Asian, African, native Indian, and Caucasian so that we may understand roots and culture of those around us, and to expand our awareness and intelligence

6 STEPS TO CONVERT TO RASTAFARI
Step#6
Accept yourself as a Rasta

Accepting yourself as a Rasta means seeking no validation from others. This was so hard for me to accept when I first started my journey as a Rasta, because I yearned for somebody to pat me on the back and say "nice job, you are doing the right thing." The truth of the matter is this experience never happened, and this experience will probably never to you either.

Every Rasta knows that to embrace Rastafari is a personal journey so you will have to give that *pat on the back* to yourself. You will just have to *know* based on hard facts, and the life and wisdom of other Rastafari, that Rastafari *is* the right spiritual choice for you, and simply accept yourself as being what you were born to be...a Rastafari.

Rastafari clothing to Convert to Rastafari

Dressing as a Rastafari will work wonders to help you feel more Rastafari. You will now choose clothing that are *Rastafari colored*. This means clothing that are predominantly Red yellow green black and white.

Faces and Symbols on Rasta Clothing

There are some very specific people whose <u>faces and symbols</u> may be on t-shirts for example, that may also be considered "Rastafari clothing" too regardless of what color it is in.

Dr. Martin Luther King	The Star of David
Marcus Garvey	King Selassie I
Lion of Judah (flag)	Jamaican Flag
Malcolm X	Shape of Africa
	A Crown
	Any Lion

Rasta typically *do not* wear other types of symbols (upside down crosses, skull, machine gun, cartoon characters etc.) on our clothing, *that are not Rastafari* because it may be seen as a denouncement of our faith. In other words it may be seen as a Contradiction and confusion as a Rasta. Just something to be aware of as you choose clothes to wear as a Rasta.

Rasta colors may be worn together or in separate pieces. Many Rasta feel a spiritual Joy when we wear natural Jewelry (wood, stone, shell, etc) that is inclusive of Red Yellow and green.

When I go shopping for clothes anything I can get in Rasta colors (Red Yellow and green stripes together), I buy without hesitation. Including Rasta colored socks, Rasta colored turbans, Rasta colored towels, earrings, Jackets etc.

Red Green and black are Rasta colors too because they are the colors of the Marcus Garvey Flag.

Wearing a Turban as a Rasta

When I started my Journey as a Rasta Empress I wore a turban every day. Nobody saw my locks including my family. For me at that time it just felt like the right thing to do for myself spiritually.

Also as an Empress there are certain spiritual guidelines to adhere to which demonstrate a respect for our bodies as *Instruments of Creation,* and *one who carries and houses growing life.*

Wearing a Turban as a Rasta Empress symbolizes self Respect, modesty, femininity, and a respect for Kingman as *the one whom the hair (holy dreadlocks) crown is reserved for.* In other words Rasta Empress do not wear the dreadlocks crown for sensual, or sexual attraction to other men, or to be attractive to friends and family, this is why we wrap our dreadlocks in a turban when in public places. Apart from that many Rasta, male and female, wrap their dreadlocks in a turban so that they reserve one part of themselves for Jah only. It's a personal and spiritual choice.

5 STEPS TO CONVERT TO RASTAFARI RECAP

- Throw out cow's milk, meat and any packaged food from your refrigerator
- Hang your first Lion of Judah flag
- Read the King James Version Bible to seek truth and Wisdom
- Buy and eat only organic fresh fruits and Vegetables and dried natural foods (such as dreid apples and dried apricots etc.) for snaking
- Buy and Listen to more Music by Rasta Reggae music Artists; Capleton, Sizzla, Garnet silk etc.
- Wear Rasta Colored clothing and symbols
- Wear a Turban to cover your dreadlocks if you choose

HOW TO CHOOSE YOUR RASTA NAME

So, why does Rasta change their name once they start to embrace the Rastafari Livity? The reason is to start *a new.* To commemorate the renewal of self. To tell the world that you are <u>not a Babylonian</u> any longer, and that you now Represent Jah. There for you need a *new name tgo go with the new lifestyle and to reinforce that*

you are your own person now, instead of a name that represents being a slave to Babylon lies and tricks.

King Selassie I was born *Tafari Makonnen.* When he became King of Ethiopia, the High priests <u>renamed</u> him *Haile Selassie I,* which translates to "*Power (might) of the Trinity"* this is his coronation name.

5 Tips to help you choose Your Rasta Name

1. Choose your Rasta name straight from the Bible
2. Make up a Rasta name by using some Jamaican Patois words
3. Put the word "Ras" in front of your birth name if you are a male, put the Word "Empress" or "Queen" in front of your birth name if you are a female.
4. Use a word that is part of Rastafari Culture (Jah, Trinity, Haile, Lion, etc)
5. Mix up these options

List of Rastafari words to incorporate as part of your new Rasta Name

Zion	Highly/Heights
Royal	Roots
Kingly	Mystic/Mystical
Tafari	Natty
Menen	Ascend
David	Lion
Prophet	Truth
Trinity	Jah

How I chose my Rasta Name

My Rasta name is Yuajah (Yu – are – Jah)

I chose that name for myself soon after I started growing my dreadlocks. I knew before I grew my locks I was going to have to have a Rasta name to commemorate the change of spiritual awareness in my life, from Christianity (Baptism name) to Rastafari, spiritual heights name.

I put the word "Empress" in front of my Rasta name to Emulate the name of *Empress Menen.* In Rastafari Culture most Rasta women like to put the word "Queen" in front of their Rasta name. I like Empress because it sounds more I-cient to me.

 I like my Rasta name because it is original and consists of Jamaican Patois and incorporates the word *Jah.*

Rasta men are naturally called "King." Some prefer the word "Ras" in front of their Rasta name, meaning "Prince" or "head." Again it is a personal Choice.

4 WAYS TO MEDITATE AS A RASTA

4 WAYS TO MEDITATE AS A RASTA #1

Rastafari Silence Meditation

Sitting in Silence allows one to exercise/experience them self as their spirit. Our spirit knows only love. Over time when you practice meditation in this way, you may begin to notice, your mind seems to *think less*, experience more love gratitude and acceptance and you may begin to notice the feeling of nature and the air around you.

I have heard this referred to as *stillness.* I

like to call it *oneness,* as a Rastafari because when this experience happens I become one with nature. The last time this happened to me unexpectedly my mind lost its ability to "negative chain link think." I felt free, as if I was existing as my spirit without the physical body or any awareness of negative experience, past or present.

4 WAYS TO MEDITATE AS A RASTA #2

Rastafari Rhythmic Music for Meditation

Listening to Rasta Reggae music is another great way for Rasta to "I-ditate."

Rasta Reggae music is Rhythmic. You may notice yourself losing track of time and space when you listen to this music under the right circumstances, especially if the Rasta Reggae music has drumming in it.

yhI like to listen to some Dennis Brown when I am alone or while lying on my bed late at night. The Reggae beat, and the words of the music, calm my nerves, and lift my spirit. Positive Rhythmic Reggae music is great for Rastafari meditation.

4 WAYS TO MEDITATE AS A RASTA #3

Rastafari Nature Contemplation Mediation

I usually will do *contemplation mediation* when I am having a good day and want to share my good vibes with Jah. I do it in one of two ways,

looking at nature (a large body of water, or a forest, or up at the clouds, or a light snowfall etc. Pretty much Anything that involves seeing and or feeling,

or experiencing nature, and thinking of all the beautiful properties. Or sometimes I lie down on my bed and think about all the experiences of that day.

A Contemplation meditation should be done when you are alone, once again on a day when you are feeling *a high* from good vibrations and want to share these feelings with and give thanks to, the creator. Jah loves when we contemplate his works and give him thanks.

4 WAYS TO MEDITATE AS A RASTA #4
Bible Reading for Meditation as Rasta

Bible Reading is a great part of Rastafari. You may have heard Rastafari referred to the Rastafari livity as... *a meditation*. Well, some of us Rasta feel fall into a meditative state after reading the bible. Many times those relaxing feelings last for the whole day, when the bible dis read in the morning.

As a Rasta it is important to read your King James Version bible not to understand or even to believe what's in the book but for the meditation and relaxation and wisdom it can bring as a Rastafari. Yes, bible study is repetitively mentioned in this book, because it is such an important part of being a Rasta because it overlaps and influences all else that we do and experience. Such as charity work, receiving blessings, and knowing what is acceptable to Jah.

Bible reading should be done 3 times

daily as a Rasta for Meditative Purposes as a Rasta.

How often should I mediate as Rasta?

There is no time requirement or restriction regarding mediation. However as a Messenger of Jah, I would recommend one to two hours per session at least 2 times a week at minimum, to stay grounded as a Rasta. The purpose of mediation as a Rasta is to keep Babylonian thinking at bay, and keep our spirit in line with Rastafari Consciousness.

4 WAYS TO MEDITATE AS A RASTA #5

Rastafari is a Life Meditation

The life of living as Rastafari is a meditation within its self. It is a consciousness that recognizes all life. Plants, insects, humans, planets etc. Within the framework of this consciousness, Rastafari have appreciation and toleration for all of Jah creations. For this reason Rastafari is also referred to as "a meditation" Meaning an awareness of life as a spiritual Journey.

Rastafari" Life mediation" is about being conscious that we (life) are all interconnected by one source of Love and power that is Jah.

4 WAYS TO MEDITATE AS A RASTA RECAP

- Rastafari Silence Meditation allows one to exercise his/her spirit. If done on a consistent basis the mediation may come naturally in time without effort.
- Rastafari Reggae Rhythmic Music may cause one to mediate by losing track of space and time do to the positive words and drumming
- Rastafari Nature Mediation is done looking at and feeling nature and contemplating the works of Jah
- Reading the bible on a consistent basis can bring feelings of relaxation to Rasta
- Rastafari is a Life Mediation is awareness of life as a spiritual Journey. We as Rasta practice appreciation and toleration for all Jah Creations

WHY ARE YOU A RASTA?

This section is for those new to Rastafari who may be concerned about what to say when asked "Why are you a Rasta?" Here is a suggestion on how to respond. It has two parts.

Response: "I know that King Selassie I is the King of all Kings talked about in Revelation 5:5"

"...weep not: behold, the <u>lion of the tribe of Judah</u>, the root of David, hath prevailed to open the book, and loose the seven seals..."

Response: King Selassie I crowing title

is...

"King of Kings, Lord of Lords, Conquering <u>Lion of the Tribe of Judah,</u> Elect of God."

4 PILLARS OF RASTAFARI HEALTH

In Rastafari culture, good health is an all encompassing endeavor. We believe that good health is a result of...

1. Healthy choices for the temple
2. A calm spirit and calm mind
3. Healthy relationships with others
4. A close personal relationship with the Jah

RASTAFARI HEALTH PILLAR #1

Healthy choices for the temple -

Rasta do not ingest pharmaceuticals

As Rasta we ingest everything natural as much as we possibly can. The reason is that we feel that Jah made man, and when he made man he gave them natural roots and herbs for ailments and healthy food to eat. Jah did not create pharmaceuticals. Rasta takes herbs, roots and vitamins for most health issues. Many of us have natural health and healing books readily available in our homes. Rasta knows that Babylon created pharmaceuticals to keep making people take them (keep making people sick) so that they become dependent and Babylon makes more money. As Rasta you may purchase your own health and healing book online or your local book store.

I strongly recommend having a book in your home on natural medicine to help guide you into natural medicine and healing awareness as a Rastafari.

Good health of the body is for the short and longer term as a Rasta.

RASTAFARI HEALTH PILLAR #1 continued...

Fasting for spiritual Health as Rastafari

Many people do not consider the spirit to be part of the health of the body. I can ensure the spirit is an integral part of our physical and emotional well being and should be maintained and properly "fed."

2 Reasons Rastafari fast...

Rasta fast to exercise the spirit so to speak, in the way that we halt a time when we eat so that our mind can experience our existence as the spirit instead of as a physical being, driven by physical desires. Doing this as a Rasta helps one to practice self control and to develop spiritual health and awareness.

The other reason is to provide the body a break from digesting food. Everything needs to take a break. It's just healthy and wise to do so.

Many Rasta fast from Friday at sundown to Saturday at Sundown. Some Rasta fast on Tuesdays, to honor the Ethiopian Sabbath day. As long as you fast one or both of these days, then you are covered as a Rasta, for exercising spiritual health and well being.

RASTAFARI HEALTH PILLAR #1 continued...

Rasta Temple cleanse

In the Rastafari Livity we are aware of all of the additives and preservatives that may be in our food. The typical human body does a good job of food expulsion. However because we as Rasta practice natural health care, we read and learn that the bowels could use some extra help in ridding itself of "gunk." Rasta like to do a herbal cleanse once a month, for optimal health, and to promote healthy digestion.

RASTAFARI HEALTH PILLAR #2

A healthy spirit and calm mind

Meditation is a large part of Rastafari health. Rasta believes a calm mind, leads to a calm healthy spirit, which leads to a calm healthy body.

Anything done in a relaxed state is a form of meditation. However as a Rasta we are careful to meditate *positive thoughts* instead of negative thoughts.

Meditation as a Rasta is clearing the mind, or contemplationu *in a relaxed state.* The point of it all is what you do *in the relaxed state.* Think positively!

Many Rasta like to in a relaxed state and

ponder all the beauty of Jah creations. Jah Rastafari.

RASTAFARI HEALTH PILLAR #3

A Close personal Relationship with Jah

Your relationship with Jah will take time. It is so important as part of our health as Rasta because all that man, cannot and does not provide... Jah does. Don't have any Expectations of Jah...just seek him honestly from your heart for however long it takes, and he will come to you when he knows your heart is pure.

My close relationship with Jah has helped me in so many ways. Jah helped me release anger one day when I was determined to hurt back a woman who had hurt me. Jah completely took those emotions of anger, and frustration combined with determination...away. I would have changed my whole life in one of the worst ways had I done what I wanted to do that day. Jah also *protects* his servants.

Jah helped me release emotional pain. I once had a love relationship that devastated me so much, I thought I wouldn't be able to live anymore without that person in my life. I had no appetite, I thought that I would never feel happiness again... I even contemplated suicide. I prayed to Jah and he just put a simple wisdom into my heart...

He let me know that the relationship didn't have to be *forever* for me to appreciate it. That I could appreciate the *gift of* the relationship however long it lasted and that I didn't have to blame him just because it didn't last longer. The next day I began to feel myself again, the sunshine felt good again, and I started once again to believe that good things were instore for me. Jah can do that...He has the power to help us.

As you can see, having Jah as your best

friend has its perks. If you desire to have a close personal relationship with him it just takes persistence and a sincere intention.

Jah Manifests himself in many and all ways

Jah manifests himself in other people, in experiences, in nature etc...that's why Rasta are always paying attention to what's going on around us. Because we know Jah is always around us and always in communication with us, especially when we least expect it.

To seek a personal relationship with Jah, one must seek truth. Jah is truth. Live the Rastafari Livity and seek truth...Jah is in everything at all times. When you seek truth at all times, you will run into Jah, again and again, naturally. Once you develop a close personal relationship with him, he will become your guide on the Journey of life.

RASTAFARI HEALTH PILLAR #4

Healthy relationships with others

As Rasta we know all is vibrations. In life Rasta must encounter people who are not like him, people who do not share his beliefs, and people who will be disrespectful....

Dealing with Babylonian Thinking as a Rasta

As Rasta we know that *people are not bad.* Some of us some of the times, just make unfortunate choices out of Babylon conditioning.

What should a Rasta do when he has to deal with a family member or friend who exhibits Babylonian thinking and behavior?

The Rasta has a 2 options...

1. *Keep the relationship but keep at a distance, in* order that the power of Jah may still be present in that person's life through Rastafari
2. Decide to *disconnect the relationship altogether* because the will of Satan is too strong, and we do not want to fight, argue, defend, protect etc each day because that

> type living is not Rastafari, and can cause a lower vibration mediation.

We as Rasta try very hard not to disconnect other people from our lives, whether they are "bald head" or whether they are Rasta. As Rasta we see ourselves as *teachers and messengers of the highest order.* However at the same time, we are aware that to remain spiritually healthy,h there must be *restrictions* to the types of people and relationships we maintain on the journey in order that we may keep our mind and spirit clean.

Rasta puts the duty of Rastafari first, and his own personal comfort second.

The company you keep (as Rasta)

Every Rasta has the awareness that *whom* we interact with, on a day to day basis, and about what, is an important part of health of the mind. Experiences leads to thought, thought leads to meditation, mediation influences action.

As a Rasta *the company you keep* is just as important as the food you put into your body, because the mind is a living breathing part of spiritual health.

To be "healthy" as a Rasta means one must have a healthy calm mind. If a Rasta is consistently bothered by his/her family and or friends a calm mind will be hard to achieve and hard to maintain.

Rasta choose wisely, who they call their "close personal friends," and the type of conversation and or activities, done with these individuals. Rasta do not participate in; agreeing to hurt others, to lie on behalf of another, to laugh or mock another etc. due to friendship or wanting to impress a particular person. We *are not* of Babylon and therefore Satan cannot use us.

Rasta maintains healthy friendships with those who respect our faith, respect themselves and respect other people.

FOUR PILLARS OF RASTAFARI HEALTH RE-CAP

- Part of "health" as a Rasta also means, healthy Relationships with others
- The most important part of Rasta health, is a close personal relationship with Jah
- Good health is about wise choices, A calm mind helps Rasta to make wise decisions.
- A healthy and clean temple (body) is important because the temple is part of spiritual health as Rasta

ITAL FOOD AS RASTA

Eating food as a Rasta means giving ithanks to Jah and enjoying the food he has given us to eat *as* naturally as he has given it to us to eat it.

Jah instructs Rasta to eat food that is...

High in nutritional value

Natural

That will promote strength and vitality

Ital food is Zion food

Jah foods are Zion foods. Zion food or Ital food as Rasta call it, is natural colorful clean, healthy, and good for people to eat. In Zion, food is picked from a tree, reaped from the earth, peeled with the teeth etc. Rasta like to eat the same way they know they will enjoy foods in Zion.

Clean eating leads Rasta to Zion

Babylon has many foods available but not all are for Rasta. In Rastafari we see our temple as a large spiritual instrument. Rasta believe clean foods lead to a clean body, a clean body leads to a clean mind, a clean mind leads to clean thinking and clean thoughts lead to Zion.

Rastafari prayer of thanks Giving

When Rastafari prepare to eat food, we always say a prayer of thanks to Jah before we begin. We know all good things come from Jah and that Jah is our provider. Jah *loves* to be praised. Rasta say thank you to Jah as eating food is one of the greatest enjoyments and blessings to mankind.

Rastafari Prayer Before Eating

"Oh Jah, Bless this food that you have provided for I and I. Thank you Jah. May this food provide I and I with health and Strength…give thanks for life.

Jah Rastafari"

Which foods are forbidden for Rasta?

- Fish *without* scales
- Pork (bacon, pepperoni etc)
- Beef
- Cow's Milk / Goats Milk
- Table Salt (Sea Salt is ok sparingly)
- Shell fish
- Alcoholic beverages

Many of the rules regarding food and eating as Rasta may be found in ``Leviticus`` in the King James Version Bible.

Many Rasta in Jamaica don't even want any fish on their plate. They refer to it as "deaders."

Ital food is Jah food

The first 3 times I cooked without salt and ate the food, I didn't enjoy it all. I realized once I stopped obsessing about salt in my food there were other ways to enjoy food besides flavor. *They are called Texture, Color* and *natural flavor.*

Jah is so amazing. I remember eating some Ackee and enjoying the texture of it in comparison to the other food on my plate one day. I really began to "overstand" that Jah is in all things, we simply need to experience it natural (Ital) to get the full enjoyment.

What is the big deal with Rasta and Salt Anyway?

Let me explain to you plainly. Everybody is at a different levels spiritually. Salt in a Ital food diet, will not help the temple to attract Jah. It takes away from the natural experience of eating the food which <u>would</u> attract Jah. Some Rasta can feel spiritual things…for those Rasta, a little thing such as eating salt in the food, takes away from the spiritual Heights one can feel in eating food….which many people don't see as a spiritual act. However it is a spiritual act...you simple need to acquire the right spiritual heights to know it.

What types of foods should I as Rasta eat?

Jamaican Earth (Ground) Food used In Ital Cooking

Pumpkin	Cho-cho
Yam	*Cassava*
Plantain	*Irish Potato*
Cocoa	*Sweet Potato*
Dasheen	
Green Banana	**These foods are typically boiled, fried, baked or roasted in Rastafari.*
Bread Fruit	

Common Jamaican Vegetables used in Ital cooking

Calaloo	*Pop Choy*
Squash	*Carrot*
Cabbage	*Cauliflower*
Lettuce	*Broccoli*
Okra	*Radish*
Ackee	*Turnip*
	Beet Root

Fruit Eaten By Rasta in Jamaica

Mango	Sour sap
Plum	Sweet Sap
Apples	Custard Apple
Water Melon	
Bananas	Cherries
Grapefruit	Coconut Jelly
Lucas	Star Apple
Tamarind	Star Fruit

Legumes often used in Jamaican Ital Food cooking

Red Peas	String beans
Goon go peas	Sugar beans
Snow peas	Split peas
Cow Peas	Black eyed peas
Jerusalem Red peas	Lentils
Kidney beans	Chick peas
Broad beans	Peanuts
	Often used to in stew, rice and peas, soup

*Many Rasta avoid the use of black pepper for seasoning, because it doesn't break down in the body .

How to Season Ital food as Rasta

There are about 10-12 different types of *seasonings* commonly used in Rastafari Ital Jamaican style cooking. I would like to introduce you to them, now that you will be cooking your food without salt. They may be used in any combination on any foods you wish, including fish, chicken or Veggie chunks.

Keep in mind when I say "seasoning" I am not talking about the kind you buy in a package or a small *shake out* container. Jamaican Rasta are referring to *natural food spices* when they refer to "seasoning,"

Jamaican Seasoning and Spices used in Ital food Cooking

Thyme	Pepper
Tomato	Pimento
Scallion	Lemon Grass
Scotch Bonnet	Curry Powder
Honey	Garlic
Lime	Ginger

ITAL FOOD AS RASTA RE-CAP

- Rasta drink No alcohol
- Rasta use natural food for seasoning (garlic, ginger, pimento etc.)
- Rasta say a prayer of thanks Giving before eating food
- Rasta do not eat shell fish
- Rasta eat only fish *with* scales
- Rasta do not eat Red meat (pork, beef, goat etc)
- Rasta eat a variety of fresh organic vegetables and earth foods, and dried snacks

6 SPIRITUAL OBLIGATIONS OF RASTAFARI

Rastafari spiritual Obligation #1
To Help the poor & the needy

As Rasta we do not *turn our eyes away* from the poor and needy in an attempt to pretend they do not exist. Rather it is our spiritual duty as servants of Jah, to help the poor and the needy.

How can Rasta help the poor and the those in need?

Donating used clothing to second hand

stores that helps those less fortunate by selling quality used clothes for men women and children; for less.

Donating our time, perhaps as a volunteer in a homeless shelter or a local soup kitchen

Donating money to Charity. However if you choose to go this route try to donate personally to a needy person. Jah likes to see his servants interacting with and showing love for his creations personally.

Another Reason Rasta help the poor and the needy is to receive Jah Blessings. Jah Jah is the creator. He loves to reward his servants with blessings. You will only know once you begin helping the poor and the needy.

Rastafari spiritual Obligation #2 To "Serve Jah"

Rasta are servants of Jah. We see our self as living extensions of Jah in Babylon. We cannot be selective about the work we do. Jah does not *conditionally* love and conditionally serve. We must serve unconditionally too, all of Jah creations. The poor the needy, the elderly, the white, the black, the Babylonian and the Rasta. Any person can be a person in need.

Rastafari spiritual Obligation #3
To Seek Truth

As Rasta it is your spiritual obligation to seek truth. You have to know in Babylon as Bob Marley said "half the story has never been told." Babylon tries to hide the truth from all of us. But Jah made Rastafari and through us the truth shall be revealed.

As a Rasta seeking truth means, doing research. Rastafari is the heritage and truth of all people not just Ethiopians. It is your responsibility as a Rasta to find out and learn what Babylon is hiding from you.

As a Rasta the truth, is our purpose. It is what we defend. Truth, equal rights, and justice. Seeking truth in all things including, food ingredients, historical events, rumours about others etc. To seek truth is one of the major pillars of developing a Rastafari consciousness.

Rastafari spiritual Obligation #4
Keep the Holy Sabbath in Honour of Jah

The 10 Commandments state

<u>Remember the Sabbath day and keep it holy...</u>

That implies that Jah knows many of us will <u>forget</u> the Sabbath day and won't understand what it means to keep it holy. Rasta keep the Sabbath every Friday from sundown till Saturday until sundown. To keep it holy means to keep it clean. No swearing, no sex, no partying with friends on the Sabbath day.

According to Rastafari God Rested on the 7th day it was a Saturday not a Sunday. But if you ask me I would say rest Saturday and Sunday too if you can.

Rastafari spiritual Obligation #5
Honour Jah

The Reason Rasta Keep a Sabbath is to Honour Jah. We reserve a special day, just for him. On that day we clean our homes, cook a special Ital meal, do not go to work, read a chapter of the King James Version bible, keep our television turned off until 5:00pm...all Just for Jah.

So what do Rasta do during the Sabbath for entertainment?

Most play Rasta Reggae music, organize the home for the week to come, read some conscious literature about Africa, or Nelson Mandela, or create some Rastafari inspired Art or poetry, or spend the day with our significant other reasoning about life and or the bible. Spending one day with Jah, doing what he has requested of me, feels really good. Not all Rasta honour the Sabbath day, but many still do.

Rastafari spiritual Obligation #6 Develop a Rastafari consciousness

By releasing certain thoughts and habits and engaging in certain spiritual practices combined with accepting certain beliefs and releasing other beliefs, A Rastafari consciousness may be achieved. A great book to read to learn about this is called....(Egyptian...)This is a two step process.

Maintain a Clean temple: For example, Smoking Cigarettes and Drinking Alcohol gum up the holy temple and therefor spiritual connections to Jah his wisdom and understanding.

Develop a Love for Jah creations: We as Rasta accept that we are one with all beings and there for have love for all of Jah creations including tiny insects. This is demonstrated in Rastafari when we refer to ourselves as "I and I" and speak of others as "The I" we mean that it is the *spirit self* that connects us all and that we are referring to when we use these words.

A Rastafari consciousness takes time and effort to achieve in totality. Once you embrace it as who you already are, you will begin to see how Jah works with you to achieve the desired goal.

As Rastafari Messengers of Jah we aim to ....
- **Release:** Anger, Hatred, Jealousy, Envy, Fear, Judgment etc.
- **Embrace:** Love, Forgiveness, Creativity, Faith, Gratitude, Unity etc.

In order to develop and maintain a consciousness fitting for a Queen or a King.

- As Rasta we aim to release anger and embrace love
- Rasta know we are one with all beings so we have love for all Jah creations
- Rasta keep the Sabbath on Saturday Just for Jah
- Rasta are truth seekers. This includes food ingredients, historical study, listening to both sides of a story
- Rasta serve Jah by helping the poor the needy, and the eleder whenever the need arises
- Develop a Rastafari consciousness.

6 SPIRITUAL OBLIGATIONS OF RASTAFARI RE-CAP

1. To develop a Rastafari consciousness
2. To honour Jah
3. To keep the Holy Sabbath in honour of Jah
4. To Seek truth
5. To Serve Jah
6. To help the poor and needy

BIBLE STUDY AS A RASTA

Do I have to Read the bible as a Rasta?

As a *Rasta you are not obligated to Read the bible.* However as a Messenger and teacher of Rastafari, I must make known to you that not reading the bible will not bring you any closer to Jah, and will allow Babylon to fill your mind with corruptive thoughts.

Bible study as a Rasta is done as more of a mediation of "overstanding" more than anything else. You don't have to believe in it, you just need to read it for the spiritual transformation it will give you over time.

Which bible does Rasta Read?

Rasta read the King James Version Bible. The reason is that we feel the bible is constantly being altered to remove cultural references and historical facts that bring one into unity with Jah, and that provides one with wisdom. Rasta knows the King James Version bible is typically older, and includes stories of many prophets including...

- Moses
- Nahum
- Daniel
- Ezra
- King David
- Samuel
- King Solomon
- Etc

We as Rasta, feel the Kings James version bible is more complete and demonstrates

Rastafari culture throughout. Read and pay attention for yourself. There are references to "locks, turbans, Sabbath, feasts, Babylon, Kings, beards, special diets," etc.

The King James Version bible also provides written documentation of what was told to the prophets to tell to the people. If one wants to know the rules of life according to Jah Rastafari, he may read and study the King James version bible.

Why do Rasta Read the bible?

Jah words have a certain vibration. When we read them in a relaxed state with a clean heart, we may feel a spiritual vibe of *oneness* with the creator. This happens for me all the time. It begins to happen when I let go of the obligation of reading the bible and just read it for the interest of the stories and literature.

How often should a Rasta read the bible?

A Rasta should read his or her bible 3x daily.

- I read my bible in the morning 10-15 minutes before I leave the house.
- 10-15 minutes when I come back into the house
- 20-30 minutes at night before I go to bed.

This is the right amount to keep our mind as Rasta on the desires of Jah, and keep Babylon thinking at bay. You may begin to notice a positive change in your thinking and your behaviors too.

What if Bible Reading doesn't fit my schedule?

Rastafari is a very flexible mediation. If you cannot stick to the schedule of reading your bible, simply adjust it. Jah will not be vex with you for that. He cares that you do it every day as much as you can...consistently.

BIBLE STUDY AS RASTA RE-CAP

- You do not have to read the bible to be a Rasta
- Rasta Read the King James Version bible because it has more detailed and accurate truth, from various prophets
- Rasta Read the bible for the Meditation it gives
- A Rasta who chooses to read the bible should read it at least 2 - 3 times daily

WHITE RASTAFARI

There is no "Rastafari for white people" only, Rastafari taught with the white Rasta in mind.

In Rastafari all people regardless of skin color are invited to embrace Rastafari. Between true Rasta there is no skin color only love and overstanding.

How are White Rasta viewed in Rastafari?

White Rasta are seen as special beautiful and wise. Why? Because it is *common* in Babylon to believe that God is white, especially when one is white themselves. Many Rasta who are African feel flattered by white Rasta and want to get to know more about them. Many Rasta may ask many questions such as... How did you come into the Rastafari way of life? What bible do you read as a Rasta? How old were you when you locked your hair? etc. Other Rasta see white Rasta as a compliment to our faith. The more Rasta in the world, the better the world will be.

Rastafari is a Multinational Faith

In Rastafari there is no skin color just people who seek truth, know the truth and wear dreadlocks in honour of that truth. In Rastafari we are all one nation That nation is Love.

WHITE RASTAFARI RE-CAP

- There is no such thing as *White Rastafari*
- There is no skin color between Rasta people only love
- White Rasta are seen as special in Rastafari and a compliment to the faith

JAH RASTAFARI

THE MEANING OF DREADLOCKS AS A RASTA

Dreadlocks represent Life and Love

Dreadlocks are the representation of the Rasta covenant with Jah. *You can think of dreadlocks as wedding bands shared between a husband and a wife who have taken vows of love, commitment, and fidelity.* As a Rasta the dreadlocks are an outward representation that symbolize love for Jah, the creator of heaven earth and all life.

Dreadlocks Represent Natural living

Dreadlocks also represent a love for nature and natural living. Below are some Keywords associated with Rasta Dreadlocks.

Spirit	Zion
Jah	King Selassie I
Purity	

Self Discipline Fidelity Cleanliness Ancestors Creation Africa	Empress Menen Love Truth Africa Unity Nature

How to wash your Dreadlocks as Rasta

As Rasta we like to use natural products for bathing and grooming. Our Dreadlocks are no exception. Rasta likes to use natural shampoos from the natural health and beauty shop to wash our spiritual crown.

What does the Aloe and Lime mixture do for Locks?

The aloe and lime mixture helps dreadlocks to form when they are new and stay firm at the root. Many Rasta use the mixture when coming out of the shower. You just rub it into the hair at the root and on the locks when the locks are wet, go about your day as usual and the aloe and lime mixture will over time lock the hair.

Be sure if you do choose to use the aloe, make sure there are no tiny bits of the aloe skin in your mixture. Use a strainer. You don't want aloe bits showing as you go about your day, in your gorgeous Rasta dreadlocks.

How to grow dreadlocks as a Rasta

The most spiritual and organic way of growing your locks as a Rasta is to allow them to form on their own. No twisting, nor braiding no going to the hairdresser....just let the locks form on their own. Some people do prefer a more uniform "neat" look for their locks and part them neatly at the root and use a *latchhoook* for tightening the roots. You will have to know which method best suits your lifestyle and your desires.

Once your dreadlocks begin to grow you can wrap them under a turban, wear a crown, otherwise known as a "dreadlocks cap" or wear them loose. Whichever suits you best.

The outward appearance of the dreadlocks as Rasta, symbolizes an inward change, of thought and mind, to higher awareness of Jah Rastafari consciousness.

THE MEANING OF DREADLOCKS AS RASTA RE-CAP

- The way to grow dreadlocks as a Rasta is organically. Just allow them to form on their own over time
- Rasta use a mixture of Lime and Aloe to lock Dreadlocks
- Rasta was their dreadlocks using natural shampoos and conditioners from the natural health and beauty shop
- Dreadlocks represent natural living, life, and love

OVERSTANDING JAH ZION & BABYLON

Who is Jah?

Jah is a spiritual entity. He is not in human form, however he can manifest himself any way he wishes, including in human form, and he does have a spiritual vibration. What you are about to read is something that every Rastafari knows. *Jah has a vibration of an African.* If you could feel him. His vibration, he would feel

African.

Jah is very loving and very powerful. He is omnipresent and so forgiving. He created human beings to love him and to trust him and to have a relationship with him all the days of our lives.

What is Babylon?

Babylon is the world we live in now. It is talked much about in the King James version bible, "The beast of Babylon" etc.

Here are some common traits of Babylon society and living.

- Lies
- Corruption
- Sexual Perversion
- War
- Poverty
- Hatred
- Fear
- Abuse of Power
- No fear of Jah

Rastafari talk allot about Babylon and their tactics against anybody who represents truth, such as Rastafari. Babylon's *God* is Satan. All vanity and materialistically and sexually driven thinking and living. Babylon is where we live today in all parts of the world.

What is Zion?

Zion is what many Rasta people call heaven, Zion is the same earth we live in now (Babylon), after Jah Jah has cleaned it up and removed all the wickedness, corruption and the Babylonians. Zion is a perfect place where Jah roams. One must be invited into Zion in order to Enter. Only those who seek Jah and live by his commandments and do his work are invited into holy mount Zion.

In Zion there is only ...

- Peace
- Love
- Righteousness

- Jah

One Key to draw closer to Jah

Coming close to Jah can take years. But it is well worth the blessings that you receive and the relationship with him *is in comparable to anything else in this life.*

One key to coming close to Jah is to live in

righteousness. Jah loves those who serve him and who live brotherly and sisterly with others. Holding grudges and getting people back for pain they have caused is Satanic behavior under Rastafari. Live Jahly and open up your heart. Jah sees and knows all things. When he sees that you are reading his holy book and doing his work, in his own way he will draw closer to you.

OVERSTANDING JAH ZION AND BABYLON RE-CAP

- "Getting people back" when they have wronged you is Satanic behavior under Rastafari
- Zion is earth once it has been cleansed by Jah
- One must be "invited" into Zion to see it. Rasta will be judged by Jah according to his works/deeds
- Babylon is the earth we live in today where Satan rules and roams
- Jah is a spirit entity. His vibration is African. He can manifest himself in any way including in human form
- Living in righteousness may draw one closer to Jah over time

Babylon is the of the physical realm, Jah seateth in Zion and is of the spiritual realm. The awareness of Zion can be exercised through developing a Rastafari consciousness and way of living.

HOW TO RAISE A RASTA CHILD

In Rastafari children are treated like gold by their Rasta parents. Young babies are newly birthed living and breathing creations of Jah. They have the potential to be *great.* We as parents simply need to plant the seed of Rastafari in their lives for them to want to embrace the faith and become a beacon of light who inspires others.

It's not so much about Raising them as Rasta, its more about inspiring them to want to inspire others, positively through whichever avenue they choose. Rastafari is one of those avenues. Rasta never force a child to embrace Rastafari if it is not of their desire. In those cases we keep our minds focused on inspiration as a Parent of Rastafari Livity.

To lock or not to lock? (dreadlocks and Rasta Children)

Some Rasta parents believe they should lock their children's hair for them from birth. Some Rasta parents believe it should be the childs choice whether or not to lock the hair. I say when the child reaches age 3 start locking the hair as a Rasta parent. When the child turns age 11-13, give them the option to follow Rastafari or to follow Babylon. By that time they will have the *overstanding* that Rastafari is the spirituality of their parents, and of what Babylon living is all about.

Let them make the decision once they are old enough to decide. When they are too young, keep them close and put Jah covenant on their head.

Deep down no Rasta parent wants to have a bald head child but we respect other peoples right as individuals *to choose* even if it is our own child.

Be a Living Example of Jah love

The most powerful influence one has for raising Rasta children is one's self. children's minds are like a sponge. If you want to raise your child as Rasta, it is important that you do all the things one is supposed to do as a Rasta within your own life and home. Rasta Parents must demonstrate themselves as a living *Examples of Jah Love* at all times, so that our children will want to emulate our behavior, and there for will emulate Rastafari.

As a Rasta parent it is important that we show our children an abundance of ...

- Love and affection
- Patience and understanding
- Respect for their journey
- Understanding of their blunders
- Wisdom and spiritual devotion

Rasta parents respect their children because we know they are Jah creations. They have recently manifested in the flesh, and have come here to learn and to grow.

Rasta children must see their Rasta parents reading the King James Version bible on a daily consistent basis so that they too will know that it is important to read the King James Version bible.

When Rasta children grow up and experience life for themselves, they will know the power of Jah for themselves because through their parents they have seen a living example of the livity their whole lives.

Television and Raising Rasta Children

Many deep Rasta do not allow their children to watch television. I would do the same, because I do the same for myself now – I don't watch TV. Many people are totally unaware of the power of the television on the subconscious mind and the way it programs, our beliefs, desires and actions.

Alternatively

- Rasta parents provide videos, books, games etc. about African and Caribbean Roots and culture to their children, Including food, history, people, language art etc. For their children's learning and entertainment.
- Rasta parents sit down with our children daily and read them books and or literature about history including the history of black slavery, and the history of other nations
- Rasta parents provide their children with a King James Version bible so that they may read and learn about the stories of the bible and the prophets in their own time.

5 Rasta Beliefs to teach your Rasta child

1. All cultures and nations and their beliefs and way of life are equal to yours and significant
2. That King Selassie I and Empress Menen are our role Models as Rasta people.
3. That the creators name is *Jah* and that King Selassie I is his Elect
4. That all people are *Africans* because the first man Jah created was a black African, there for all people are African because we share the same ancestral root.
5. That Zion is our home as Rasta, and that we must live clean and righteous to enter Zion.

Because Rastafari is not a Religion, raising a Rasta child, is more about sharing the light of Rastafari with your child, until they come of age to acknowledge the teachings of Rastafari on their own.

HOW TO RAISE A RASTA CHILD RE-CAP

- Rasta parents should teach their Rasta child to inspire others positively
- Rasta may "Lock" the Rasta child's hair until they are age 11-13 then let them decide if they want to start their own set of locks or live as a bald head
- Many Rasta parents don't allow Rasta children to watch TV. Instead they spend time with them reading books and watching DVDs, about other cultures.
- Rasta parents should teach their children that Zion is our home as Rasta, and that we must live clean and righteous to enter

FINDING A RASTA MENTOR

1. *Are you a Rastafari?*
2. *What makes you a Rasta?*
3. *Have you ever considered not being a Rasta?*
4. *What does King Selassie I mean to you?*

5. *What is your opinion of Zion and Rome (Heaven and Hell) as a Rasta?*

There is no right or wrong answers to these questions. I designed them to give you a more in depth look into the *consciousness* of the potential Rasta mentor.

Here are the questions you should be asking yourself about your mentor as you get to know him/her and absorb/observe their lifestyle as a Rastafari.

Does this mentor answer the same question, asked many times, regarding the faith, the same every time?

For example; *what is your duty day to day as a Rasta?*

Does this mentor keep the faith tight?

Does he/she eat strictly Ital food?
Does he/she read the bible daily?
Does he/she speak positively of people?

More questions to ask *yourself* about your Mentor

Does he gossip about others?
Does he/she refrain from certain habits/foods/behaviors?

>...one night stands?
>...smoking cigarettes?
>...drinking alcohol?
>...eating red meat?

Does he/she put an end to arguments occurring in his presence?
Does he/she call the name of the King Selassie I or Jah early in the morning or in "thanks giving?"
Does he/she refer to himself as a messenger/servant of Jah?

What if I can't find a Rasta mentor?

If you are having a hard time finding someone to be your Rastafari Mentor.... try leaving a message on Rastafari message boards and forums online saying you would like some guidance on the livity. Many deep Rasta enjoy guiding others into the faith.

Becoming a Rasta Mentor Yourself

These abilities will not happen overnight, they will require much introspection and reasoning with other Rastafari. A Great place to start ``reasoning`` as a Rasta is on a website called rastafarispeaks.com

You will know you are ready to become a Rasta mentor when...

- You can answer questions pertaining to Rastafari the same on a consistent basis without consulting a book or thinking too long and hard

- When you see yourself as a servant of Jah and have concrete *works* to substantiate your faith.

- When you overstand spiritually why you abstain from certain foods, habits, and practices as a Rasta.

- When you can sum up the purpose of your life as a Rasta in few words.

Rastafari is not just a faith, it is a way of life (a Livity) inclusive of duty. Only you will know why you have been called by Jah, and have also chosen to respond to the call. It takes time (in most cases years) to leave the old way of life and thinking (as a Babylonian) and become a strong and a deep living example of Jah Rastafari.

FINDING A RASTA MENTOR RE-CAP

- You will know you are ready to be a Rasta mentor after you have been a Rasta for some years

- To find a Rastafari Mentor go online to Rastafari message boards and ask for someone to be your mentor. Rasta love to share the livity with others

- Ask your Potential Rasta mentor many questions about the faith, and observe their behavior to make sure they practice what they preach

KING SELASSIE I SPEECHES

Leadership – By King Selassie I

Leadership does not mean domination. The world is always well supplied with people who wish to rule and dominate others.

The true leader is a different sort; he seeks effective activity which has a truly beneficent purpose. He inspires others to follow in his wake, and holding aloft the torch of wisdom, leads the way for society to realize its genuinely great aspirations.

The art of leadership is in the ability to make people want to work for you, while they are really under no obligation to do so. Leaders are people, who raise the standards by which they judge themselves and by which they are willing to be judged. The goal chosen, the objective selected, the requirements imposed, are not mainly for their followers alone.

They develop with consumate energy and devotion, their own skill and knowledge in order to reach the standard they themselves have set.

This whole-hearted acceptance of the demands imposed by even higher standards is the basis of all human progress. A love of higher quality, we must remember, is essential in a leader.

The true leader is one who realizes by faith that he is an instrument in the hands of God, and dedicates himself to be a guide and inspirer of the nobler sentiments and aspirations of the people.

He who would be a leader must pay the price in self-discipline and moral restraints. This details the correction and improvement of his personal character, the checking of passions and desires and an exemplary control of one's bodily needs and desires.

To be first in place, one must be first in merit as well.

He who has not learned to render prompt and willing service to others will find it difficult to win and keep the goodwill and cooperation of his subordinates.

A leader will kindle interest, teach, aid, correct and inspire. Those whom he leads will cooperate with him in maintaining discipline for the good of the group. He will instruct his followers in the goals towards which to strive, and create in them a sense of mutual effort for attaining the goal.

The Bible – By King Selassie I

WE IN ETHIOPIA HAVE ONE OF THE OLDEST VERSIONS OF THE BIBLE, but however old the version may be, in whatever language it might be written, the Word remains one and the same. It transcends all boundaries of empires and all conceptions of race. It is eternal.

No doubt you all remember reading in the Acts of the Apostles of how Philip baptised the Ethiopian official. He is the first Ethiopian on record to have followed Christ, and from that day onwards the Word of God has continued to grow in the hearts of Ethiopians. And I might say for myself that from early childhood I was taught to appreciate the Bible and my love for it increases with the passage of time. All through my troubles I have found it a cause of infinite comfort.

"Come unto Me, all ye that labour and are heavy laden, and I will give you rest" who can resist an invitation so full of compassion?

Because of this personal experience in the goodness of the Bible, I was resolved that all my countrymen should also share its great blessing and that by reading the Bible they should find truth for themselves. Therefore, I caused a new translation to be made from our ancient language into the language which the old and the young understood and spoke.

Today man sees all his hopes and aspirations crumbling before him. He is perplexed and knows not whither he is drifting. But he must realise that the Bible is his refuge, and the rallying point for all humanity. In it man will find the solution of his present difficulties and guidance for his future action, and unless he accepts with clear conscience the Bible and its great Message, he cannot hope for salvation. For my part I glory in the Bible.

Spirituality – By King Selassie I

The temple of the most high begins with the human body, which houses our life, essence of our existence. Africans are in bondage today because they approach spirituality through Religion provided by foreign invaders and conquerors. We must stop confusing religion and gspirituality. Religion is a set of rules, regulations and rituals created by humans which were supposed to help people grow spiritually.

Due to human imperfection religion has become corrupt, political, divisive and a tool for power struggle. Spirituality is not theology or ideology. It is simply a way of life, pure and original as was given by the Most High. Spirituality is a network linking us to the Most High, the universe and each other. As the essence of our existence it embodies our culture, true identity, nationhood and destiny. A people without a nation they can really call their own is a people without a soul. Africa is our nation and is in spiritual and physical bondage because her leaders are turning to outside forces for solutions to

African problems when everything Africa needs is within her. When African righteous people come together, the world will come together. This is our divine destiny.

Living in Peace – By King Selassie I

Wise men have always known the deep and pervading truth that it is better to give than to receive, for even as it conflicts with selfish and ambitious desires, it moderates and controls them.

Giving always demands sacrifice. To overcome the temptation to enjoy mere daily comfort, to press resolutely and patiently forward on the scheduled way, are true tests of the high degree of determination that should bind you together. Memories of past injustices should not divert us from the more pressing business at hand.

We must live in peace with our former colonizers, shunning recrimination and bitterness and fore-swearing the luxury of vengeance and retaliation, lest the acid of hatred erode our souls and poison our hearts.

Let us act as befits the dignity which we claim for ourselves as Africans, proud of our own special qualities, distinctions, and abilities. We must speak out on major issues, courageously, openly and honestly, and in blunt terms of right and wrong.

If we yield to blandishments or threats, if we compromise when no honourable compromise is possible, our influence will be sadly diminished and our prestige woefully prejudiced and weakened.

On this day which men of earth and angels of heaven could neither have foreseen nor known, I give thanks unutterable by the mouth of man to the living God who has enabled me to be present among you.

Today is the beginning of a new era in the history of Ethiopia. Since this is so, do not reward evil for evil, do not commit any act of cruelty like those which the enemy committed against us. Do not allow the enemy any occasion to foul the good name of Ethiopia.

We shall take his weapons and make him return by the way he came.

We believe in cooperation and collaboration to promote the cause of international security, the equality of man and the welfare of mankind.

We believe in the peaceful settlement of all disputes without resorting to force.

And in accordance with the charter of O.A.U. we will strive to eradicate colonialism, racism and apartheid from the face of the earth, to frustrate the efforts being made by foreign powers to dictate the destiny of the African continent, and we will continue to stand.

A New Way of Life – By King Selassie I

What we seek is a new and a different way of life. We search for a way of life in which all men will be treated as responsible human beings, able to participate fully in the political affairs of their government; a way of life in which ignorance and poverty, if not abolished, are at least the exception and are actively combatted; a way of life in which the blessings and benefits of the modern world can be enjoyed by all without the total sacrifice of all that was good and beneficial in the old Ethiopia. We are from and of the people, and our desires derive from and are theirs.

Can this be achieved from one dusk to the next dawn, by the waving of a magic wand, by slogans or by Imperial declaration? Can this be imposed on our people, or be achieved solely by legislation? We believe not. All that we can do is provide a means for the development of procedures which, if all goes well, will enable an increasing measure and degree of what we seek for our nation to be accomplished. Those who will honestly and objectively view the past history of this nation cannot but be impressed by what has already been realised during their lifetime, as well as be awed by the magnitude of the problems which still remain. Annually, on this day, we renew our vow to labour, without thought of self, for so long as Almighty God shall spare us, in the service of our people and our nation, in seeking the solutions to these problems. We call upon each of you and upon each Ethiopian to do likewise......

Above all, Ethiopia is dedicated to the principle of the equality of all men, irrespective of differences of race, colour or creed.

As we do not practice or permit discrimination within our nation, so we oppose it wherever it is found.

As we guarantee to each the right to worship as he chooses, so we denounce the policy which sets man against man on issues of religion.

As we extend the hand of universal brotherhood to all, without regard to race or colour, so we condemn any social or political order which distinguishes among God's children on this most specious of grounds.

The Essence of Power – By King Selassie I

The power which you possess is but one side of the coin; the other is responsibility. There is no power or authority without responsibility, and he who accepts the one cannot escape or evade the other. Each one of you and each servant of the Ethiopian nation and people would do well to ponder these words, to take them to his heart, and to guide his conduct in accordance with their teachings. This is the challenge which faces you today. Let your labours here during the coming year demonstrate your capacity to meet it.

May Almighty God guide and assist you in your work.

MY RASTA JOURNEY

My Friend Ras Anthony insists I should put my "Rasta Story" in this book. He feels sharing my Rasta journey will give others an inside look into Rastafari.

Growing up Christian & Becoming an Empress

Rastafari just always *felt right* for me. I was raised as a Christian, and for many years I saw myself under *that light.* As I matured certain "things" "Rasta things" just felt right for me. Such as listening to Rasta reggae music, eating Ital food, not eating any more meat or pork, and learning about African culture and history. Finally through Rastafari I was able to find myself and my truth.

Growing my natty Dreadlocks Crown

At age 31, I decided to lock my hair. I felt totally comfortable with my decision but felt totally uncomfortable carrying out the deed. Knowing that Jah is truth... I pressed on.

Rastafari Helped me to Love Myself...Completely

On October 22nd 2008, I freed myself through Rastafari. I pulled out all of the synthetic braids (hair extensions) from my hair and allowed my own natural hair to form into dreadlocks. I also began wrapping my locks in a turban style head-wrap. I finally could *feel* myself and unexpectedly fell in love with myself. It was as if wearing fake hair and hiding my own hair, wasn't allowing me to love myself totally. I became all me from head to toe after 20 years of braids, weaves, chemical hair straigheteners and wigs, under the power of the Almighty Jah...and it felt right.

My first *Works* as a Rasta

During the early months of my Journey, Jah inspired me to write a book on Rastafari. I didn't know anything about writing a book or how to go about publishing it, but I decided to go ahead and do what Jah was asking me to do.

That book is now published and is called *how to become a Rasta*. It is my first book of about 7 books on Rastafari that I have written. Writing that book and publishing it was good for my soul. The greatest reward is that now as a Rasta I can point to my *works,* something every Rasta likes to have to follow in the footsteps of King Selassie I and Empress Menen. Such works are otherwise called "Legacy" in Rastafari, or "Jah works."

Every Rasta Journey is Unique

Every Rasta journey is unique, every Rasta has their own relationship with King Selassie I, and Jah the creator. Don't expect your Journey to be like mine. Expect Jah to guide you, as his unique servant, in his own way, in his own time.

Talk to him at anytime for any and all reasons, and allow him to unfold his works through you in your life.

My Life as a Rasta Woman today

I continue to write Rasta books today. My life is Rastafari, from the food I eat, Ital, to the books I write Rastafari (check out my Rastafari fiction stories too "Dr.Love; for better or for worse" coming in February 2016) Jah has blessed me with the ability to sing and DJ Rasta Reggae music also.

One of the greatest blessings Jah has allowed me to experience happened on January 25 2016.

I got married to a Kind humble caring Kingman. He is my soul mate. We are raising his 4 year old Rasta child together. *Give Thanks and praises Jah Rastafari.*

Always remember to share love as a Rasta

Living in love as an Empress has taught me so much. Consider doing the loving thing towards another person when they anger or frustrate you. Watch how it changes the energy between the two of you.

I hope some of what I experienced and have shared with you in this book as an Empress will be helpful on your Rasta Journey.

Blessed Love, May the Journey of Rastafari strengthen and inspire you. King Selassie I.

If you have any questions or comments, please visit me at my blog jamaicanrastafarianlove.com. or visit amazon.com and leave a comment about the book. I would love to hear from you.

Jah Guidance, and Jah Love.

MORE BOOK TITLES BY EMPRESS YUAJAH

- Rasta Way of Life (Best Seller)
- Rastafari for African Americans
- Life as a Rasta Woman
- How to become a Rasta
- Rastafari Beliefs and Principles
- Rasta Bible

ABOUT THE AUTHOR

Empress Yuajah continues to write books on Rastafari culture. She is now writing fiction books about Rastafari characters. Her first fiction novel is entitled "Dr. Love, for better or for worse" to learn more about her and her books, visit www.jamaicanrastafarianlove.com

EMPRESS YUAJAH

JAH RASTAFARI